A CeNTuRy OF CHANGE

Transport

Jane Shuter

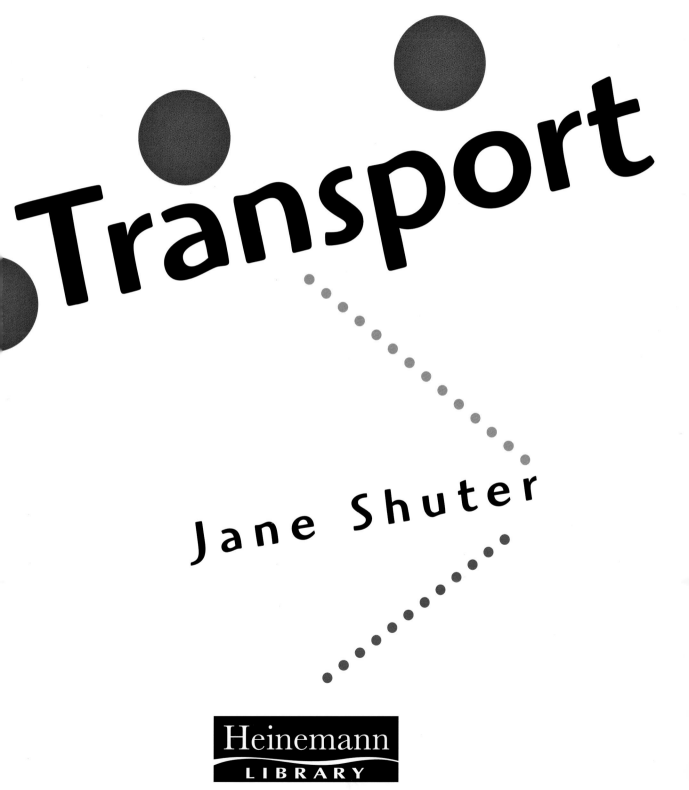

Heinemann
LIBRARY

First published in Great Britain by Heinemann Library,
Halley Court, Jordan Hill, Oxford OX2 8EJ
a division of Reed Educational and Professional
Publishing Ltd.
Heinemann is a registered trademark of Reed Educational
& Professional Publishing Ltd.

OXFORD MELBOURNE AUCKLAND
JOHANNESBURG BLANTYRE GABORONE
IBADAN PORTSMOUTH (NH) USA CHICAGO

Designed by Celia Floyd
Originated by Ambassador
Printed in Hong Kong/China

03 02 01 00 99
10 9 8 7 6 5 4 3 2 1

ISBN 0 431 03878 3

British Library Cataloguing in Publication Data

Shuter, Jane
    Transport. – (A century of change)
    1. Transportation – Great Britain – History – 19th
       century – Juvenile literature
    2. Transportation – Great Britain – 20th century –
       Juvenile literature
    I. Title
    388'.0941'09034

Acknowledgements
The Publishers would like to thank the following for
permission to reproduce photographs:

Corbis, p. 4; Corbis-Bettman, pp. 6, 10, 12; e.t. archive,
p. 20; Image Bank, p. 5 Andy Caulfield, p. 7 John P Kelly,
p. 27 Erik Simonsen; Mary Evans Picture Library, p. 24;
National Motor Museum, p. 8; Popperfoto, pp. 14, 16,
18, 22; Quadrant Picture Library, p. 15, p. 21 Paul
Sherwood; Robert Harding Picture Library, pp. 11, 13,
17, 23; Science Photo Library, pp. 28, 29; Telegraph, p.
19 Malcolm Fife; Tony Stone, p. 9 Martyn Goddard, p. 25
Ross Harrison Koty; Wright State University, p. 26.

Cover photograph reproduced with permission of Tony
Stone/Martyn Goddard and the National Motor Museum.

Our thanks to Becky Vickers for her help in the
preparation of this book.

Every effort has been made to contact copyright holders
of any material reproduced in this book. Any omissions
will be rectified in subsequent printings if notice is given
to the Publisher.

For more information about Heinemann Library books,
or to order, please telephone +44 (0)1865 888066, or
send a fax to +44 (0)1865 314091. You can visit our
website at www.heinemann.co.uk

Any words appearing in the text in bold, **like this**, are
explained in the glossary.

CONTENTS

By 1900, people were able to travel further than ever before. They were no longer limited to the distance they could walk or a horse could go. There were many new forms of transport. Although motor cars were only used by the wealthy, bicycles, trains, trams and buses were cheap enough for lots of people to travel on.

Trips and holidays

Cheap train travel meant that many more people took trips and holidays by 1900. They went to places, such as seaside resorts, that only well-off people visited before. Some people even went abroad.

Helping people travel

One of the first travel agents was the Englishman Thomas Cook. He organized his first Grand Tour of Europe in 1856. His success encouraged W. F. Harden to start a similar US travel company called American Express. By 1900, both companies were organizing trips all over the world. They are still successful businesses today.

New and old forms of transport jostle each other in Chicago in 1905. You can see horse-drawn vehicles, pedestrians, motorized vehicles and electric trams.

Today, modern transport enables people to travel longer distances as part of their daily life. People use cars, buses, trains, the underground and even planes to get to and from work.

Trips and holidays

People go further and faster on more trips and holidays than they did 100 years ago. The first successful short flight by an aeroplane was not until 1903, but there are now fifteen airports across the world that serve over 20 million passengers a year, and hundreds of other airports that serve over a million passengers a year.

Getting to work

A 1998 survey showed that people spent about the same amount of time travelling to work as they did in 1900, but were travelling much further. The average distance travelled in 1900 was 6 km, and about half of all workers walked to work. In 1998 the average distance was 10 km and only 2 per cent walked to work – the rest used cars or public transport.

Changing the world

The development of different kinds of transport has changed the world we live in. Cars, buses and trains have altered the appearance of the countryside. Suburbs have grown as people have moved out of the cities, knowing that they can use their cars or public transport to get to work. Houses and even blocks of flats are built with garages for cars. Many people now work in the transport industry. But most importantly, nowhere seems very far away now that you can travel halfway round the world in 10–12 hours.

Despite the fact that they use a lot of fuel and cause a lot of **pollution**, more people are making plane trips several times a year.

Improved models

By 1900, bicycles were a common sight on roads in Europe and the USA. They were a dramatic improvement on the early pedal cycle that had been invented by Scotsman Kirkpatrick Macmillan in 1839. The new bikes had improvements, such as brakes, gears for hill-climbing and air-filled rubber tyres. But they were still quite heavy, so most riders ended up pushing their bikes up steep hills, not riding them.

Lady cyclists

When bikes were first invented they were seen as an invention for male use. Some companies made ladies' tricycles, which were like chairs with a wheel at each side and at the front.

By 1900 it had become acceptable for women to ride bikes and there were special cycling skirts available. They were like baggy trousers with one long, full section for each leg.

A craze for cycling

Because bicycles had become cheaper, safer and easier to ride, there was a craze for cycling by 1900. The arrival of the safety bicycle, first manufactured in Coventry in the 1880s, had made bikes available to almost everyone.

In New York in the 1890s there were special schools where people could be taught how to ride a bike.

Today's cycles

Bikes have improved greatly since 1900. The frames are lighter and stronger, and the tyres are not so likely to puncture. The design of the seat and handlebars makes cycling more comfortable, and better gearing makes it easier too.

Mountain bikes

The tough off-road cycles known as mountain bikes were developed in the late 1960s and early 1970s in California in the USA. The first mountain bikers were motorcyclists who were no longer allowed to ride their motorbikes on off-road dirt trails through the mountains. Some of the early mountain bikes even had motorcycle handlebars. These first mountain bikes looked so tough but basic that they were known as 'clunkers'.

Bunny-hopping

At first mountain bikers developed all sort of tricks to get over the obstacles they came across as they rode up and down rough mountain tracks. These skills helped them avoid injuries and win races. Now, some of these tricks and stunts are performed as part of competitions. One of the most famous stunts is the bunny-hop, which is like jumping while on a bike!

Mountain biking is fun for everyone, allowing people to cycle in places that early cyclists could never have reached.

The first petrol-driven four-wheel car was built in 1885 in Germany. Early cars were made to order and cost about five times an ordinary person's yearly wage. Most people used horse-drawn vehicles or trains for long journeys.

Teething troubles

Cars were faster than horse-drawn vehicles. But they were open to the wind and rain, so the people inside could get cold, wet and even muddy. The drivers and passengers dressed in special 'motoring' clothes such as thick jackets and goggles. Early cars were also not very reliable. Spare parts were hard to get. There were not many garages or trained mechanics.

People who bought cars were told how the cars worked, and were expected to do their own repairs.

A danger to the public?

The first cars on British roads had to follow the same rules as steamrollers. In towns the speed limit was only 5 km/h. Someone had to walk in front of the driver with a red flag to warn of danger. In 1896 a new law set a town speed limit of 8km/h and the red flag rule was dropped.

Henry Ford's first 'horseless carriage' appeared on the streets of Detroit, Michigan, USA, on 4 June 1896. It could only go at two speeds – 16 and 32 km/h.

Today, many people think that life without a car would be impossible. People have changed the way they live and work because of the car. People live further from their work than they could have 100 years ago. Modern cars are faster, so people can take a day trip to places that people in the 1890s could never have reached in one day.

Better – and worse

Cars are now more reliable. It is easier to buy fuel and spare parts, and to get repairs done. Roads are better and there are more of them. But the success of the car has caused problems. The huge numbers of cars on the roads in some areas causes air **pollution.**

In some cities, like Tokyo in Japan, there are days when the air is so bad that cyclists and pedestrians are advised to wear masks to filter the air they breathe. At 'peak times' when many cars are on the roads, there can be huge traffic jams. In Athens, the capital city of Greece, cars with even license numbers are let into the city on some days and those with odd numbers on others. It is hoped that this will cut down the city's traffic. Traffic jams can lead to 'road rage'. This is when people get so frustrated by driving conditions or the cars around them, they lose their tempers and become violent towards other drivers.

This Bugatti was built in the 1990s and can reach a top speed of 280 km/h.

Faster, cheaper travel

The British were the first to use railways and to provide cheap, fast transport for passengers and goods. The first passenger railway opened between Stockton and Darlington in 1825. The first railway to link major cities was the Liverpool and Manchester railway in 1830, a journey of 53 km. At the end of 1830 there were 80 km of track in Britain. By 1900 there were over 34,500 km of track.

Railways quickly spread all over the world. Early trains were powered by **steam engines.** The coal that was burned to make the steam made rail travel smoky and sooty.

But engineers were already experimenting with cleaner ways to power trains. In Germany William von Siemens was working on an **electrical rail** to run trains. **Diesel engines** were also being developed. By 1900 **electric engines** started to be used on some specialized services.

Rails link an empire

Between 1850 and 1907 the British spent over £8 million building 962,892 km of railway tracks around the world. It was useful to link different parts of the British Empire, and to carry the goods they traded with it. It also carried administrators, messengers and soldiers.

By 1900 railways had been built across the continent of North America and engineers had to design bridges and tunnels for them to run along.

New 'Age of the Train'

By the mid-20th century most trains around the world had changed from steam to diesel and electric power. At the beginning of the first 'Age of the Train' passenger trains could only travel at about 40–50 km/h. Now, the Japanese Shinkansen bullet train regularly speeds along at 210 km/h. The French high-speed train, the TGV *(Train à Grande Vitesse)*, has reached a top speed of 290 km/h and often travels at speeds of over 220 km/h.

Flying trains

One of the new methods being used to power trains is **magnetic levitation.** Maglev trains float above their special tracks on an invisible magnetic cushion. Magnetic fields propel the train along above the track. Because the train does not touch the track, there is no friction to slow it down.

Experimental maglev trains in Japan and Germany have recorded speeds of more than 400 km/h.

Railways today

Most countries in the world now have more kilometres of railway track than they did in 1900. Britain is one of the few exceptions. The USA has the most track of any country, but almost all of the trains that use the tracks carry goods and not passengers.

The Japanese bullet train is one of the fastest types of train in regular service.

Why have underground trains?

Trains were very good at linking towns and cities together. As cities grew bigger, people wanted to be able to travel quickly by train from one part of a city to another. Ordinary railways could not be built because the cities were already full of roads and buildings. So engineers developed ways to put railways in tunnels running underneath the cities.

Who had underground railways by 1900?

The first underground railway, the 6 km Metropolitan and District Railway, opened in London in 1863.

Steam engines pulled the carriages. It was dirty and smelly, but was so successful that it carried 9,500,000 passengers in its first year. By 1900 the London Underground system had several lines working on the much cleaner electric **traction** system. Other cities around the world quickly took up the idea. There were underground railway lines in New York City in 1868, Budapest in 1896 and Boston in 1897. The first 10 km stretch of the Paris Metro opened in 1900.

This photograph of the interior of Marble Arch station in the London underground system was taken in 1890.

Learning from the past

Today, many cities around the world have underground systems. New underground systems benefit from the mistakes made in the older systems. The underground in Bilbao in Spain opened in 1998. It used the latest engineering and construction technology to make the trains and passenger waiting areas light and spacious, and as easy to clean as possible. The lines are clearly laid out and easy for everyone, including foreign visitors, to understand.

The Tokyo underground system was built in 1927. At rush hours it is the most crowded underground with 164,000 passengers.

Where's the driver?

In the 1970s the first remote-controlled underground trains were introduced. A section of the Victoria Line on the London Underground was designed for automatic trains in 1971. The first complete system to use automatic, computer-controlled trains was the Bay Area Rapid Transit System in the San Francisco Bay area of California, USA, which opened in 1976. All of the trains are operated by remote control, using technology borrowed from the **aerospace industry**. Most new systems are now air-conditioned, faster and give a smoother ride because of better tracks and carriage-**suspension**

Modern art

Underground stations today are much more pleasant than the smoky tunnels of only 150 years ago. On the Moscow Metro, which first opened in 1935, each station is different. Some are very up-to-date with modern art designs. Others are decorated in a grand style, and even have chandeliers. The London Underground has tried to make travel on the 'Tube' less boring for passengers by introducing posters with poetry on them. These poems have become so popular that they have now been published as a poetry collection

Horse power

The first buses were like large carriages, drawn by horses. From the 1850s, many places had steam-powered buses that could travel down any road. Some towns had electric trolley buses that ran on the roads, but these had to be attached to overhead electrical cables for their power.

By 1900 many towns and cities had set up bus services. Buses on organized bus services followed specific routes, going down the same roads at the same times each day.

Because so few people owned cars, bus travel was very popular in towns and cities, and in the countryside to travel between towns.

Petrol power

The first buses that ran on petrol were developed in the early 1890s in Germany. The first service using **petrol engines** had buses that carried only eight passengers.

By 1895, when this photo was taken, even people in the countryside had regular bus services.

A thing of the past?

At first, it seemed that the development of the petrol engine was a big step forward for buses. Buses with petrol engines were cheaper to run, could travel faster and broke down less often. But cheap petrol engines were also used in cars, and as cars became less expensive more people bought them and stopped using public transport.

Most big towns and cities still have bus services, usually running on diesel fuel, but many services to rural areas in **developed countries** have been stopped. In **developing countries**, particularly Africa, bus travel is still very popular. In some places it is the only form of transport, except for walking, available to most people.

Pollution-free

Some scientists are developing buses with the 21st century in mind. In Vancouver, Canada, some experimental buses are being powered by fuel cells, which are like batteries.

They burn the gas **hydrogen** to produce electric power. Fuels cells, which are almost **pollution**-free, were developed for use in spacecraft and military vehicles. If the buses are successful, cars that use fuel cells may be developed.

In other countries, scientists have developed fuels for buses that are not pollution-free, but come from easily grown crops or waste materials. In Brazil, a form of liquid fuel has been made from sugar cane, and in the US maize oil fuel is used by some local bus systems.

Modern bus companies try to attract customers by providing toilets, videos, tea, coffee and snacks, even beds for really long journeys.

Early Trams

The first trams were pulled by horses and looked very similar to horse-drawn buses. The horse pulled the tram along tracks called tramlines. It was thought to be easier to pull a vehicle along iron rails rather than through mud and potholes.

Steam-powered trams were quickly introduced. They could go faster and carry more people than the horse-drawn trams. However, the coal burned to produce the steam power made these trams dirty and smelly.

Electric trams

In 1843, an American, Thomas Davenport, built a small electric motor and used it to power a small tram on a short stretch of track.

In 1860 another American, G. F. Train, opened three lines in London and one in Birkenhead. By 1879 trams were introduced that ran on electricity picked up from an **electric rail**. But people walking over the track could get electrocuted if their feet touched the rail. Trams were then fitted with devices to pick up electricity from under the street.

Overhead wires were also used. This was the safest system, but if the wind blew the wires down, or if they were hit by birds or tangled in tree branches, the electricity could get cut off and the trams would stop running.

A horse-drawn tram in London.

The end of the line?

As the popularity of the motor car increased so the demand for trams decreased. A tram's journey was restricted by where the tracks were laid whereas a car could go anywhere the driver wanted. By 1960 there were no more working tram systems in Britain. Although, many European cities, and some in the USA and Australia, still used trams. But people wanted the freedom that cars allowed.

The Manchester tram system links the suburbs and the airport to the city centre.

Return of the tram

The popularity of the car led to overcrowding and congestion on Britain's roads, especially around big cities. The electric tram seemed like an ideal way of travelling in and around large cities. Unlike buses, trams would not be held up in traffic jams. Trams had the advantage of being able to carry more people than buses or cars. Trams were also able to get further into the city streets than a train could. Many cities, such as Manchester, set up new tram networks.

A vital transport link

In 1900, water transport was still important for moving goods. Rivers and **canals** were especially useful for carrying heavy goods, like coal and bricks. Almost all long-distance journeys taken by people or goods used some form of water transport.

Steam rules the waves

The first practical steam-driven ships were river boats developed by the American Robert Fulton in the early 1800s. By the 1850s steam power had replaced sail power. Improvements in engine design during the next 50 years meant that by the early 1900s, steam ships were quick and efficient. In 1850 it took fourteen days to cross the Atlantic in a ship powered by a combination of sail and steam. By 1900 the journey took five days.

Luxury for some

The great Atlantic Ocean liners of 1900 were luxurious and impressive boats. The rich passengers travelling in first class had all of the comforts of the best hotels.

Passengers with the cheap **steerage** tickets, many of them **emigrating** from Europe to the USA, ate and slept together in open areas, usually in the bottom of the ship, and were not allowed to mix with the other passengers. Their food was often nothing more than porridge for breakfast and a thin stew for dinner. Between 1900 and 1920, about 12,600,000 people left Europe to start new lives in the USA.

By 1900 perishable food could be transported from one country to another in refrigerated ships like this one.

Not so fast now

Although modern ships are much faster and more efficient than ships in 1900, far fewer people travel by ship. Most people choose to travel abroad by plane.

VLCCs

For most of the 20th century the biggest ships were the military aircraft carriers used by the navies of different countries. Aircraft carriers are big enough for small aeroplanes to land and take off from their decks. Today, the biggest ships in use are called VLCCs. This stands for Very Large Crude Carriers. These oil tankers carry crude (unrefined) oil. A fully loaded VLCC can weigh up to half a million tonnes, and most are about 350 metres long. The crew often find it quicker to use bicycles rather than walking from one end of the deck to the other!

Tanker troubles

Large ships with large loads mean big problems if anything goes wrong. Tankers carrying fuel sometimes have accidents which have the most appalling consequences for the environment. Oil spills **pollute** the sea and also do a lot of harm to wildlife in the sea, or on the shores where the oil is washed up. In the last 50 years, two of the biggest disasters were the wreck of the *Torrey Canyon* on the southwest coast of England and the wreck of the *Exxon Valdez* in 1989 off the coast of Alaska.

Despite being the largest ships on the seas, tankers do not need large crews because much of their equipment is controlled automatically.

Waterways

In 1900 a lot of heavy goods were still moved around along **canals** and rivers. **Barges** were the best kind of boat for this work. They are wide and flat-bottomed, so could cross quite shallow water and could carry heavy cargo without sinking down too far into the water.

Ports

By 1900 many countries **imported** goods. Some towns on the coast became important ports where goods ships unloaded. Rotterdam, in the Netherlands, which had been a busy port since medieval times, developed into one of the largest and busiest ports, which it still is today.

Road and rail

Railways were also being used to transport goods. But, like the canals and rivers, they were of the most use to the places they passed.

In 1900 road transport was slow, but it had the advantage that there were roads to almost everywhere there were people. But only the most important roads were paved and it was difficult for heavily-laden vehicles to travel on dirt and gravel roads, particularly if the surfaces had been damaged by the weather or overuse.

In 1892 ships, roads and railways all played a part in the transport of goods in the busy city of Chicago, in the USA.

Moving goods today

Today, railways are still used for carrying goods, especially when the speed of delivery is not vital. Major rivers, such as the Mississippi, Rhine, Nile and Amazon, are also still used as a slower form of goods transportation. But in **developed countries** the roads systems, with multi-lane motorways that bypass the built-up areas of towns and cities, have become much more important. Throughout the USA, Europe and Australia, large lorries, some pulling more than one trailer, travel long distances carrying goods. In Australia there are huge 'road-trains' in which one very powerful lorry pulls a number of trailers cross-country by road – just like a train pulling several carriages.

Aeroplanes are now used to transport letters and parcels, as well as perishable goods like flowers, fruits and vegetables. Fresh foods that were only available at certain times of the year are now in our shops all year round.

Too many roads?

Today, large areas of countryside throughout developed countries are criss-crossed by paved roads. The increase in car ownership and the transport of goods by road continues to increase the pressure to widen or build more roads. But there is a price to pay for the convenience of road transport. Vehicles on roads cause air, noise and light **pollution**. Building roads involves the destruction of the countryside, and the loss of **habitats** for wildlife. A lot of traffic on roads with high speed limits can lead to fatal accidents, especially when large lorries collide with smaller vehicles. All of these problems have to be weighed up against the advantages of road transport.

Large, multi-laned roads mean that a lot of goods are now transported in huge lorries.

Fire engines ... then

In 1900 there were few types of emergency vehicle. Fire engines with **petrol engines** existed, but outside the big cities and towns some fire engines were still pulled by horses. By this time most fire engines carried about six men with axes, a tank of water, ladders and buckets. One of the fire-fighters had to clang a bell as the engine drove through the streets to warn people to get out of the way.

Police ... then

In 1900 police forces did not have many vehicles. In country areas the police still travelled by horse, bicycle or on foot.

In cities and towns some cars were used but most police were on foot or bicycles. The police could only contact each other by blowing on special loud whistles. People had to shout out or run round to a police station if they needed help.

Ambulances ... then

Ambulances were in use by 1900, but only on battlefields to transport the wounded. Some had petrol engines, but were pulled by horses. They did not have any special equipment, but were made so that stretchers could go directly inside with the lying-down wounded.

The Fire Brigade from Studley in Wawickshire, photographed in 1905 with their fire-fighting equipment.

Today in most **developed countries** there is a special telephone number to dial to get in touch with the emergency services. Most emergency vehicles are specially made for the job they do, with sirens and flashing lights to warn traffic and pedestrians to keep out of the way.

Fire engines ... now

Fire engines are now faster and bigger than in 1900. They can carry more water and also a special foam that can cover and put out chemical fires. Large cities with tall buildings have fire engines with **hydraulic** ladders that can carry fire-fighters high up the sides of buildings. Fire engines carry breathing apparatus for entering smoke-filled buildings. They also carry emergency medical equipment and cutting and lifting gear.

Police ... now

Most police now use cars, motorcycles, helicopters, jeeps and vans to get around. They have radios to keep them in touch with each other and their headquarters. Many police vehicles have special features such as bulletproof glass.

Ambulances ... now

Modern ambulance services collect injured and ill people from wherever they are, by road and sometimes by air. They carry equipment that did not exist 100 years ago. Patients in an ambulance can have oxygen, blood transfusions, cardiac resuscitation and even minor operations performed by qualified paramedics. Ambulances are now like miniature hospital casualty departments. Lives are often saved because treatment can start immediately, in the ambulance.

With the amount of traffic on today's roads it is important that emergency services can attend an accident as quickly as possible.

Just a dream?

By 1900 most people thought that the idea of reliable, safe air travel was just a dream. People made balloon flights, but they were slow and a balloon only went where the wind took it. Most people thought the future of piloted flight would be in some kind of powered balloon. In 1900 the German inventor Ferdinand von Zeppelin made a large **hydrogen**-filled balloon, powered by two engines. These 'zeppelins' were soon used for military purposes and luxury passenger travel.

In 1936 a Zeppelin was made called the *Hindenburg*. It was designed to carry 50 passengers. On 6 May 1937, disaster struck. The *Hindenburg* burst into flames and exploded, killing 36 people.

From that moment the Zeppelin was no longer considered to be competition for the aeroplane.

Early helicopters

Another development in air travel has been the helicopter. The idea of a helicopter has been around for centuries. The famous artist Leonardo da Vinci (1452–1519) made designs for a flying machine which are very similar to a helicopter. But it was not until 1907 that Frenchman Paul Cornu successfully flew the first helicopter. It was only during and after World War II that helicopters became more widespread.

The *Hindenburg* airship was introduced in Germany in 1936 as a regular transatlantic passenger service.

Straight up into the air

Today, helicopters are particularly helpful anywhere that space for take off and landing is limited. They are often used by the military and by emergency services.

Police helicopters are usually fitted with heat-seeking equipment. This is so that missing persons, suspects or escaped prisoners can be detected and followed from the air. The person's body heat is picked up by the sensors so police on the ground can be guided to the correct location.

The late 20th century has also seen the invention of the first fixed-wing aircraft that can take off and land vertically. These military planes are called jump jets. The exhaust from the engines is pushed down out of swivelling nozzles for take off. The nozzles then change position to push the aircraft forwards.

The rotary wing on top of a helicopter lifts it and propels it forward.

Airships to return?

The slowness and dangers involved in travelling by airships meant they never really made an impact on transport in the 20th century. However, they do have advantages such as their lack of noise and **pollution**. A redesigned airship system that conserves the expensive **helium** gas and makes use of a **Global Positioning System** (GPS) satellite to chart its course might well come into common use in the 21st century, according to David Windle, Future Transport correspondent for *The Sunday Times*, reporting in 1998.

A dangerous business

Many early inventors died trying to develop their flying machines. Even when the designs worked and the machine flew, the experiments were dangerous. Otto Lilienthal, the German inventor who successfully developed the glider, died in a gliding accident. Americans Orville and Wilbur Wright were influenced by the success of Lilienthal. By 1902 they had successfully tested a piloted glider. In 1903 Orville flew their famous engine-powered flying machine for twelve seconds near Kitty Hawk in North Carolina, USA.

Flyer 1

The Wrights first aeroplane was called *Flyer 1*. It was a **biplane** and had a wing span of 12.3 metres. The longest flight made in *Flyer 1* covered 260 metres in 59 seconds.

Louis Bleriot

In 1909 a Frenchman, Louis Bleriot, made the first international flight. He crossed the English Channel from France to England. His historic 37-minute flight was made in a plane he designed himself, *Bleriot XI*. It was a **monoplane** with a wingspan of 7.8 metres and a top speed of 75 km/h.

The Wright brothers' aeroplane, *Flyer 1*, could fly at about 11 km/h.

Today, it hardly seems possible that the wood and canvas planes of the 1900s could have developed so quickly into **aerodynamic**, jet-powered airliners carrying over 600 passengers. A modern jumbo jet airliner could carry *Flyer 1* on less than one half of one wing. These giants of modern aviation are 70 metres long and 19 metres high with a wingspan of 60 metres. Their normal flying (cruising) speed is 950 km/h at a height of 11 kilometres.

Faster than sound

Another innovation of the late 20th century has been the use of **supersonic** aircraft for passenger travel. The joint UK and French-built Concorde has been carrying passengers since 1976. It cruises at Mach 2, which is twice the speed of sound (about 2170 km/h).

Taking account of the different time zones, it is possible to fly from London to New York on Concorde, arriving local time in New York earlier than the local time you left London.

Gliding to Earth

One of the most exciting aircraft in the skies today is the Space Shuttle, part of the United States space programme. It is the first reusable space vehicle. It is launched into space on a rocket launcher, travels around the Earth on its mission, and then re-enters the Earth's atmosphere and glides down to land. It is covered with special tiles that protect it from the intense heat it encounters on re-entry into the Earth's atmosphere.

Today's planes, like this Boeing 777, have autopilot and computer aided navigation.

THE FUTURE?

How will people travel in the future? There is a lot of pressure on people today to use their own cars less, to cut down on **pollution**. But for this to be successful public transport must fill the gap. Buses, lorries and diesel trains pollute the atmosphere, too. So, is there a better way of powering road vehicles than using engines fuelled by petrol or diesel fuel?

Cleaner, greener cars

Electric cars, buses and trains are going to become far more widespread in the 21st century. Seth Dunn of the Worldwatch Institute said, in *Vital Signs*, in 1997: '*As more firms make electric cars, prices will drop sharply. Improved designs will reduce the weight of batteries and increase their storage capacity, this will boost sales. Electric public transport vehicles will also increase in numbers.*'

This electric bus is being recharged after its trip around Oxford's city centre. It is plugged into the mains electricity supply.

Smarter cars?

Michio Kaku, author of *Visions*, said in 1998 that all cars of the future will be run by computers. Some cars already use the **Global Positioning System** (**GPS**) he mentions. But in the 21st century the GPS will just be one element of computer control: '*As you drive, the computer will tap into the Global Positioning System satellite, orbiting in space. This warns of roadworks and delays, so the computer can map alternative routes. The computer will have **radar** to monitor the area around the car, to warn of any danger. Traffic lights will take account of levels of traffic on the road, rather than working to a set time.*'

The most likely air travel development in the future will probably be to move out of the atmosphere and into space to hop from one point on the Earth to another. Space-hopping planes would go into space for only a short time to take advantage of the Earth's movement to travel further, much faster.

New York for breakfast?

Norman LeFave, chief executive of Dynamicar Research of Houston, Texas, predicted in *The Sunday Times* in 1998 that we will be able to use short hops into space as well as conventional flights: '*This new design of plane would travel at eight times the speed of sound, some 65 miles above the ground, although for longer flights it could travel at an altitude of 50 at higher speeds. A flight from London to New York would take just 20 minutes.*'

By the twenty-first century will humans really be able to visit Jupiter and the other planets?

Jupiter for lunch?

Freeman Dyson, Professor of Physics at Princeton University, suggested in *Infinite in all directions* in 1998 that space will be firmly part of the world-wide travel network, used for trade and travel, not just for exploration: '*A system of various kinds of solar-powered electric spacecraft would make the whole solar system as accessible for trade or exploration as the surface of the Earth was in the age of the steamships. Solar-electric propulsion is the winner in space, it lets us push speed efficiency and economy as far as the laws of physics will allow.*'

GLOSSARY

aerodynamic designed to move most efficiently through the air, with the least wind drag

aerospace industry the industry that designs probes, spaceships and spacestations

barge a flat-bottomed boat that does not go down very far below the surface of the water. They would easily overturn in waves at sea, but are good for river and canal transport.

biplane a plane with two horizontal wings on either side, connected by vertical supports

canal an inland waterway dug from one place to another. Canals are the same width and depth all along.

developed/developing countries developed countries, such as the USA, are rich, industrial countries. Developing countries began industrialization later, have less industry and are not as rich.

diesel engines engines that burn an oil-based fuel, called diesel, which is lit by compressing air. The burning gives off gases that pollute the air outside.

electric engines engines that run on electricity and do not pollute the air outside

electric rail a rail set in the ground that is charged with electricity. If you touch an electrified rail it gives you a shock, enough to kill, depending on the strength of the electricity.

emigrate to move from one country to live in another

Global Positioning System (GPS) the GPS uses several satellites that orbit above the Earth and send signals which can be picked up by special receivers installed in vehicles which warn about traffic jams, accidents, and can even plan routes from one place to another

habitats places where people and animals live

helium a gas that is lighter than air

hydraulic hydraulic ladders are lifted using water pressure

hydrogen an inflammable gas that is lighter than air

imported goods that are imported are brought into one country from another one

magnetic levitation a system where a vehicle and a rail are both fitted with powerful magnets and the vehicle is held over the rail and pushed along it by the magnetism

monoplane a plane with one horizontal wing on either side

petrol engine engines that burn an oil-based fuel, called petrol, which is lit by a spark in the engine. The burning gives off gases that pollute the air outside.

pollution dirt and waste that is put into the air or water and make it harmful to use

radar a device which sends out electro-magnetic waves that bounce off solid objects and show the shapes of the objects on a special screen

steam engine engines powered by steam that is made by burning coal, wood or coke

steerage accommodation given to passengers that paid the lowest fare

supersonic travelling at a speed greater than the speed sound travels at

suspension suspension in a vehicle is a moving part underneath it that makes the bumps of the road less noticeable inside the vehicle

traction pulling something from one place to another, this can be done by several kinds of engine

INDEX